Grandma on Board

Written by Lisa Thompson
Pictures by Craig Smith and Lew Keilar

Captain Red Beard's grandmother was very excited. She was having a vacation. She was spending a week on her grandson's ship.

"Oh, it's going to be a wonderful week at sea. It's just what I need," she cried.

"Make yourself at home," said Captain Red Beard.

"Thank you," said Grandma. She walked around the ship taking notes.

"This is a wonderful ship," she said at dinner. "But there are a few little things that need changing."

"What kind of things?" asked Captain Red Beard.

"Just little things," said Grandma. "It needs a woman's touch. This place will be shipshape in no time."

The next day, Grandma ordered all of the crew to take a bath.

"And remember to wash between your toes and behind your ears!" she cried.

On Tuesday, she made the crew roll up every rope and fix the rigging.

"Cleaning as you go helps keep it spotless you know," she said.

On Wednesday, she made them mend their clothes and darn their socks.

"Dress to impress, I always say," said Grandma.

On Thursday, Grandma held a cooking class. She made the pirates eat all of her vegetable mash.

"You are what you eat!" said Grandma. She didn't see the looks on the pirates' faces.

On Friday, Grandma ordered the whole crew to the top deck for a yoga class.

"A flexible body is a flexible mind," she said.

When the end of the week came, Captain Red Beard got up very early. He ordered the crew to get a rowboat ready. It was time to take Grandma back to shore.

"Not so fast!" cried Grandma. She drew her sword. "Where are your manners? I can't leave the ship without a goodbye kiss from my grandson."

"But everyone is watching," whispered Captain Red Beard.

"I don't care," said Grandma.

Captain Red Beard leaned over and gave Grandma a kiss.

"Thank you, Stanley. I had a lovely time," said Grandma.

The crew gasped. No-one ever called the Captain by his first name. If they did, they walked the plank.

"I'll drop by next month and help you paint the ship," said Grandma. "I think purple with pink trim would look lovely, don't you?"

Captain Red Beard and his crew sailed away on a very, very, long voyage.

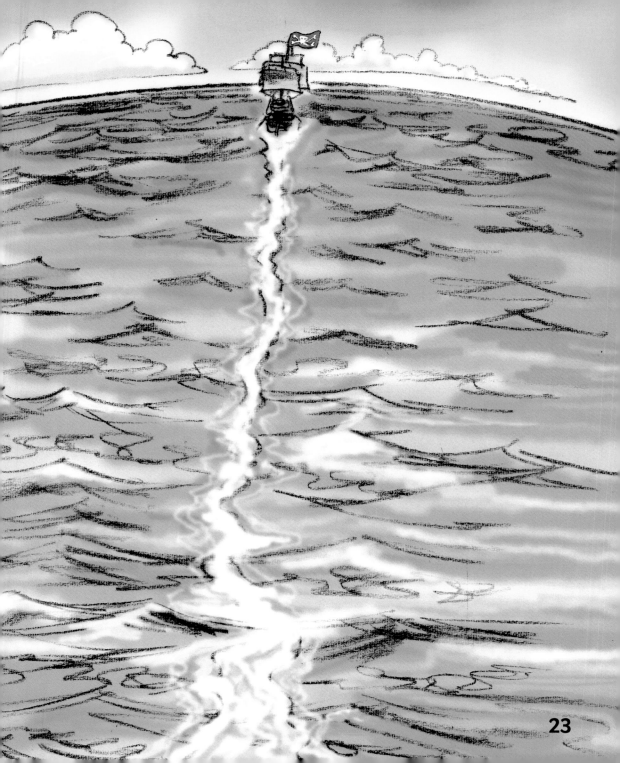